dad

bruce velick

introduction by dave barry

harmony books / new york

Published by Harmony Books, a division of Crown Publishers, Inc.,
201 East 50th Street, New York, New York 10022. Member of the Crown Publishing Group.

Random House, Inc. New York, Toronto, London, Sydney, Auckland

Harmony and colophon are trademarks of Crown Publishers, Inc.

Manufactured in Hong Kong

Design by John Fontana

Library of Congress Cataloging-in-Publication Data
Dads / [compiled by] Bruce Velick.—1st ed.
   1. Fathers—Pictorial works.   I. Velick, Bruce.
   HQ756.D36   1994
   306.874'2'0222—dc20   93-14523
                                                                      CIP
ISBN 0-517-59585-0

10 9 8 7 6 5 4 3 2 1

First Edition

dedicated to my two dads,
bernie and dave

it's 6 P.M., and we're waiting for our twelve-year-old son, Rob, to return from a quick bike ride. We're going to go out to dinner to celebrate the fact that, for the 1,000th consecutive night, we had figured out an excuse not to cook at home.

We're locking up the house when a young man comes to the door and asks if we have a son.

"There's been an accident," he says.

"Is it bad?" Beth asks.

"There's blood everywhere," he says.

* * * * * *

Sometimes I wonder if parenthood is such a good idea. Sometimes I envy fish and frogs and lobsters and other animals that just emit their young in egg form, then swim or hop or lobster-scoot away from the scene, free of responsibility, immune from anguish. I can remember when there was nobody in my world as important to me as me. Oh, I love other people—my wife, my family, my friends—and I would have been distraught if something had happened to them. But I knew I'd still be here. And that was the really important thing.

Rob changed that. Right at birth. When he came out, looking like a cranky old prune, he didn't cry. Beth, instantly a mom, kept saying, through her haze of labor pain, "Why isn't he crying? Why isn't he crying?" The nurse said sometimes they don't cry, but I could see that the doctor thought something was wrong, because he was trying to do something with Rob's mouth, and he was having trouble. He whispered something to the nurse and took Rob away, and the nurse kept saying this was routine, but we knew it wasn't. I stood there, wearing my goofy hospital outfit, holding Beth's hand, trying to cope with two staggering thoughts: First, I had a child—*I had a child*—and second, *maybe my child was in trouble*.

That was the most sickeningly vulnerable feeling I'd ever felt.

And I didn't even know Rob yet.

It turned out he was OK—just a little blockage. The doctor gave him back to us, and we quickly became traditional first-time parents, wrapped in a woozy cocoon of joy and exhaustion, taking a genuine intellectual interest in poop, marveling at the thrill we felt, the connection, when our son's tiny hand squeezed our fingers.

But the feeling of vulnerability didn't go away. It only got worse, always lurking inside, forcing me to accept that I wasn't in control anymore, not when I knew my universe could be trashed at any moment because of unpredictable, uncontrollable developments on this newborn comet, zooming through. When he was happy, I was happier than I'd ever been; but when he was in trouble . . . I can remember every detail of the time when, at ten months, he got a bad fever, 106 degrees, his tiny body burning, and I carried him into the hospital, thinking *I can't take this, please, let me be able to stop this, please, give me this fever, take it out of this little boy and put it in me, please . . .*

But you can't do that. You can't make it happen to you. You have to watch it happen to your child, and it never gets any easier, does it?

* * * * * *

ow Beth and I are in the car, and I'm driving too fast, but I have to; I have to see what I don't want to see. Up ahead some people are gathered on the side of the road, and a woman is kneeling—she has blood on her dress, a lot of blood—and lying in front of her, on his back, his face covered with blood is . . .

"Oh God," says Beth. "Oh God."

This is where it ends, for some parents. Right here, on the roadside. My heart breaks for these parents. I don't know that I could survive it.

Now I'm opening the door, stumbling out of the car toward Rob. He's moving his right hand. *He's waving at me.* He is giving me a weak, bloody smile, trying to reassure me.

"It's all my fault," he's saying. "I'm sorry. It's my fault."

"It's OK!" I'm saying. "It's OK!"

Please let it be OK.

"I'm sorry," the bloody-dress woman is saying. "I'm so sorry." She was driving the car that collided with Rob. He went through the windshield, then was thrown back out onto the road, forty feet, according to the ambulance guys.

"This is my worst nightmare," the woman is saying.

"I'm sorry," Rob is saying.

"It's OK!" I'm saying. "You're going to be OK!"

Please.

* * * * * *

He was OK. A broken leg, some skin scraped off, a lot of stitches, but nothing that won't heal. He'll be getting out of his cast in a couple of months, getting on with his ever-busier life, his friends, his school, his stuff; he'll be growing bigger, moving faster, this bright comet-boy who sneaked into my universe twelve years ago and is already starting to arc his way back out, further from me, from my control, from my sight.

But that little hand will never let go of my finger.

* * * * * *

I'm sorry. This was supposed to be a hilarious column about how Beth and I were getting ready to go out for a nice dinner at 6 P.M. and wound up eating lukewarm cheeseburgers at 11 P.M. on a table in the Miami Children's Hospital emergency room; and how Rob, after politely thanking a very nice nurse for helping him sit up, threw up on her, and other comical events. But this is how the column turned out. Next week I promise to return to Booger Journalism.

In closing, here's a Public Service Message for you young readers from Rob Barry, who won't be walking for a while, but can still operate a keyboard:

I know that bike helmets look really nerdy, and that was my argument. But I don't think I'll ever say that again. Make SURE you wear your helmets. And WATCH OUT FOR CARS.

This introduction was originally published in Dave Barry's syndicated column as "Uneasy Rider," in July 1993.

1 Stern J. Bramson

6 David Seymour

7 Mary Ellen Mark

10 Mark Chester

11 Edward Curtis

13 E. A. Kennedy

14 Dorothea Lange

15 Dorothea Lange

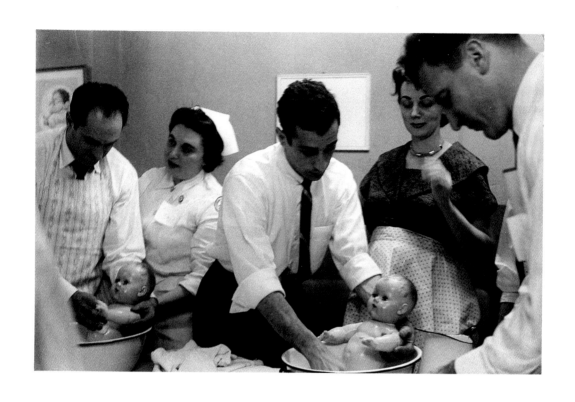

16 Henri Cartier-Bresson

17 Richard Kalvar

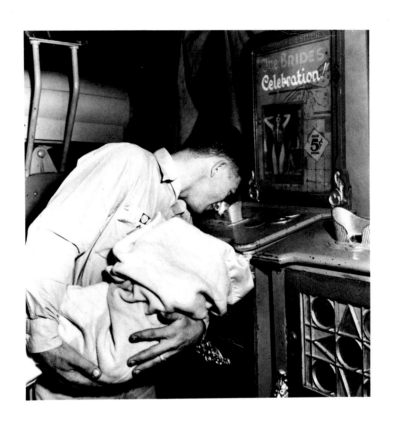

18 Ralph Crane

19 Rosen

20 Henri Cartier-Bresson

21 Abigail Heyman

22 Marc Riboud

23 Bruno Barbey

24 John Rees

25 Leonard Freed

28 Valerie Winckler

29 John Rees

30 Sebastiao Salgado

32 Thomas Hoepker

33 Sal Veder

34 François Le Diascorn

35 Jean Gaumy

36 Pierre Michaud

37 Valerie Winckler

40 Laurence Brun

41 Burt Glinn

42 Lee Friedlander

43 Jack Spratt

44 Mary Ellen Mark

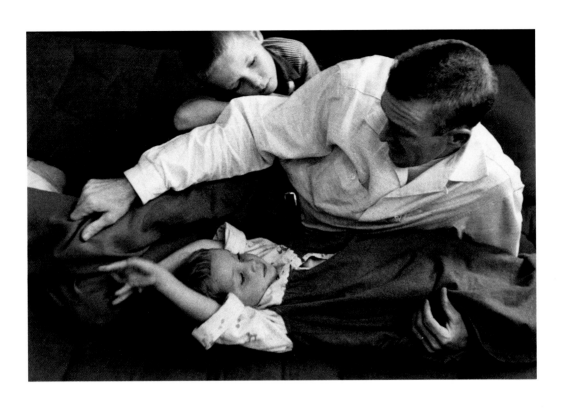

45 Eve Arnold

46 Valerie Winckler

47 Cornell Capa

48 Raymond Depardon

49 Ferdinando Scianna

52 Christophe Kuhn

53 Bruce Talamon

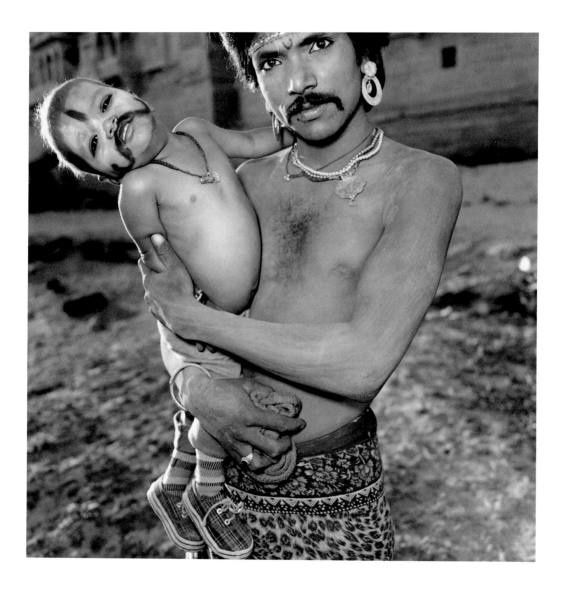

56 Thomas Hoepker

57 Elliott Erwitt

58 Mary Ellen Mark

59 Jacques Henri Lartigue

illustrations

1. Stern J. Bramson, *Four Generations of the Schuster Family*, Kentucky, 1960. (© 1988 Royal Photo Collection, Photographic Archives, University of Louisville.)

2. Joanne Leonard, Untitled, n.d. (© Joanne Leonard. Courtesy the photographer.)

3. Jean-Marc Zaorski, Alicante, Spain, n.d. (© Rapho. Courtesy Jean-Marc Zaorski/ Rapho.)

4. François Le Diascorn, *Father and Son*, India, 1980. (© François Le Diascorn. Courtesy François Le Diascorn/Rapho.)

5. Vincent Fournier, Untitled, n.d. (© Vincent Fournier. Courtesy Vincent Fournier/ Rapho.)

6. David Seymour, *The First-Born Boy in the Pioneer Kibbutz of Alma*, Israel, 1951. (© 1952 David Seymour. Courtesy David Seymour/Magnum.)

7. Mary Ellen Mark, *England 65*. (© Mary Ellen Mark. Courtesy Mary Ellen Mark/ Library.)

8.   Janine Niépce, *Le Clos de Chapitre*, Bourgogue, 1952. (© Rapho. Courtesy Janine Niépce/Rapho.)

9.   Burt Glinn, Untitled, n.d. (© Burt Glinn. Courtesy Burt Glinn/Magnum.)

10. Mark Chester, *Stockholm Archipelago*, Sweden, 1973. (© 1973 Mark Chester. Courtesy the photographer.)

11. Edward Curtis, *In a Piegan Lodge*, 1910. (Courtesy Special Collections Division, University of Washington Libraries. Photo by Edward Curtis, Negative #VW14536.)

12. Ruth Orkin, *Mary Shaving*, 1966. (© 1974 Ruth Orkin. Courtesy Mary Engel and the Estate of Ruth Orkin.)

13. E. A. Kennedy, *Homerun*, from the book *Songs of My People*. (© 1992 by New African Visions, Incorporated.)

14. Dorothea Lange, *First Born*, Berkeley, 1952. (© 1952 Dorothea Lange. Courtesy of the Dorothea Lange Collection. The City of Oakland, The Oakland Musem, 1952.)

15. Dorothea Lange, *Second Born*, Berkeley, 1955. (© 1955 Dorothea Lange. Courtesy of the Dorothea Lange Collection. The City of Oakland, The Oakland Musem, 1955.)

16. Henri Cartier-Bresson, *Red Cross Center*, Madison Avenue. (© Henri Cartier-Bresson. Courtesy Henri Cartier-Bresson/Magnum.)

17. Richard Kalvar, Untitled, n.d. (© Richard Kalvar. Courtesy Richard Kalvar/Magnum.)

18. Ralph Crane, *Sunday Outing*, n.d. (© Time Warner Inc. Courtesy Ralph Crane, *Life* magazine.)

19. Rosen, Untitled, n.d. (© Rosen. Courtesy Rosen/Magnum.)

20. Henri Cartier-Bresson, Untitled, n.d. (© Henri Cartier-Bresson. Courtesy Henri Cartier-Bresson/Magnum.)

21. Abigail Heyman, Untitled, n.d. (© 1993 Abigail Heyman/NYC. Courtesy the photographer.)

22. Marc Riboud, China, 1965. (© 1965 Marc Riboud. Courtesy of Marc Riboud/Magnum.)

23. Bruno Barbey, Untitled, n.d. (© Bruno Barbey. Courtesy Bruno Barbey/Magnum.)

24. John Rees, Untitled, n.d. (© John Rees. Courtesy John Rees/Black Star.)

25. Leonard Freed, Untitled, n.d. (© Leonard Freed. Courtesy Leonard Freed/Magnum.)

26. Eugene Anthony, Untitled, n.d. (© Eugene Anthony. Courtesy Eugene Anthony/Black Star.)

27. Wayne Miller, Untitled, n.d. (© Wayne Miller. Courtesy Wayne Miller/Magnum.)

28. Valerie Winckler, Untitled, n.d. (© Rapho. Courtesy Valerie Winckler/Rapho.)

29. John Rees, *The Grants Have Their Picture Taken*, n.d. (© John Rees. Courtesy John Rees/Black Star.)

30. Sebastiao Salgado, Brazil, 1983. (© 1983 Sebastiao Salgado. Courtesy Sebastiao Salgado/Magnum.)

31. Joanne Leonard, Untitled, n.d. (© Joanne Leonard. Courtesy the photographer.)

32. Thomas Hoepker, *JFK's Grave*, 1964. (© 1964 Thomas Hoepker. Courtesy Thomas Hoepker/Magnum.)

33. Sal Veder, *Unrestrained Joy*, California, 1973. (© 1973 Sal Veder. Courtesy Sal Veder/AP/Wide World Photos.)

34. François Le Diascorn, *France*, 1988. (© 1988 François Le Diascorn. Courtesy François Le Diascorn/Rapho.)

35. Jean Gaumy, Untitled, n.d. (© Jean Gaumy. Courtesy Jean Gaumy/Magnum.)

36. Pierre Michaud, Untitled, n.d. (© Rapho. Courtesy Pierre Michaud/Rapho.)

37. Valerie Winckler, Untitled, n.d. (© Rapho. Courtesy Valerie Winckler/Rapho.)

38. Ruth Orkin, *Father and Daughter Eating Breakfast*, Israel, 1951. (© 1981 Ruth Orkin. Courtesy Mary Engel and the Estate of Ruth Orkin.)

39. Elliott Erwitt, Untitled, n.d. (© Elliott Erwitt. Courtesy of Elliott Erwitt/Magnum.)

40. Laurence Brun, Untitled, n.d. (© Laurence Brun. Courtesy Laurence Brun/Rapho.)

41. Burt Glinn, Untitled, 1970. (© 1970 Burt Glinn. Courtesy Burt Glinn/Magnum.)

42. Lee Friedlander, Untitled, n.d. (© 1976 Lee Friedlander. Courtesy the photographer.)

43. Jack Spratt, Untitled, 1983. (© 1983 Jack Spratt. Courtesy Jack Spratt/ Black Star.)

44. Mary Ellen Mark, *Urban Poverty*, n.d. (© Mary Ellen Mark. Courtesy Mary Ellen Mark/Library.)

45. Eve Arnold, Untitled, n.d. (© Eve Arnold. Courtesy Eve Arnold/ Magnum.)

46. Valerie Winckler, Untitled, n.d. (© Rapho. Courtesy Valerie Winckler/Rapho.)

47. Cornell Capa, Untitled, 1973. (© 1973 Cornell Capa/Magnum.)

48. Raymond Depardon, Untitled, n.d. (© Raymond Depardon. Courtesy Raymond Depardon/Magnum.)

49. Ferdinando Scianna, Untitled, 1963. (© 1963 Ferdinando Scianna. Courtesy Ferdinando Scianna/Magnum.)

50. Elliott Erwitt, Untitled, 1962. (© 1962 Elliott Erwitt. Courtesy Elliott Erwitt/Magnum.)

51. Sebastiao Salgado, Bolivia, 1977. (© 1977 Sebastiao Salgado. Courtesy Sebastiao Salgado/Magnum.)

52. Christophe Kuhn, Untitled, China, n.d. (© Rapho. Courtesy Christophe Kuhn/Rapho.)

53. Bruce Talamon, *Man to Man*, from the book *Songs of My People*. (© 1992 by New African Visions, Incorporated.)

54. Mary Ellen Mark, *India Jodphur and Jaisalmer*, n.d. (© Mary Ellen Mark. Courtesy Mary Ellen Mark/Library.)

55. Robert Capa, *France: Pablo Picasso and His Son Claude in Golfe Juan*, 1948. (© 1948 Robert Capa. Courtesy Robert Capa/Magnum.)

56. Thomas Hoepker, Untitled, Illinois, 1964. (© 1964 Thomas Hoepker. Courtesy Thomas Hoepker/Magnum.)

57. Elliott Erwitt, Untitled, 1962. (© 1962 Elliott Erwitt. Courtesy Elliott Erwitt/Magnum.)

58. Mary Ellen Mark, *Urban Poverty*, n.d. (© Mary Ellen Mark. Courtesy Mary Ellen Mark/Library.)

59. Jacques Henri Lartigue, *Dani and His Son*, Paris, 1944. (© 1944 Association des Amis de J. H. Lartigue. Courtesy Association des Amis de Jacques Henri Lartigue.)

60. Monique Manceau, Untitled, n.d. (© Rapho. Courtesy Monique Manceau/Rapho.)

acknowledgments

Thanks to my agent, Candace Furhman, and my friends at Harmony Books: Peter Guzzardi, Valerie Kuscenko, and John Fontana.

Special thanks to Denise Filchner, my editor in disguise, for all her help in getting and keeping everything together.